It Must Be

Time for

Something

poems

It Must Be
Time for
Something
poems

Crystal MacLean Field

BkMk Press
Universtiy of Missouri-Kansas City

BkMk Press
University of Missouri-Kansas City
5101 Rockhill Road
Kansas City, Missouri 64110
(816) 235-2558 (voice)
(816) 235-2611 (fax)
www.umkc.edu/bkmk

Financial assistance for this project has been provided by the
Missouri Arts Council, a state agency.

Roy Fox Memorial Chapbook Series No. 6

Executive Editor: Robert Stewart
Managing Editor: Ben Furnish
Assistant Managing Editor: Susan L. Schurman
Cover photo: Jon Scott Anderson
Author photo: courtesy of Greg Field
Printing by Document Solutions, University of Missouri-Kansas City

BkMk Press wishes to thank Greg Field, Maryfrances Wagner, Warren Dinkins,
Marie Mayhugh, and Betsy Beasley.

Library of Congress Cataloging-in-Publication Data

Field, Crystal MacLean
  [Poems. Selections]
  It must be time for something : poems / Crystal MacLean Field.
  First edition.
       pages cm.—Roy Fox Memorial Chapbook Series
  ISBN 978-1-886157-86-6 (alk. paper)
  I. Title.
  PS3556.I367A6 2013
  811'.54--dc23
                    2013011602

Crystal MacLean Field's poems appeared in such journals as *New Letters*, *Chouteau Review*, *Sunday Clothes*, *Helicon Nine*, *Bloodroot*, *The Pawn Review*, *The Kansas City Common*, *Focus Midwest*, *Dacotah Territory*, *The Poetry Bag*, and *American Association of Women in Community and Junior Colleges Journal*. Her poetry was anthologized in *Kansas City Outloud* (BkMk Press), *A Change in Weather: Midwest Women Poets* (Rhiannon Press), *Missouri Poets: An Anthology* (Mid-America Press), *From A to Z: 200 Contemporary American Poets* (Swallow Press/Ohio University Press), and *Voices from the Interior: Poets of Missouri* (BkMk Press). Her previous books were *My Sister's Leather Bag* (Mid-America Press) and *The Good Woman* (BkMk Press).

It Must Be
Time for
Something
poems

I Will Not Look Away

I will not look away
from the German shepherd
belly up
like a cow
or from the small furred mass
or the blond pelt of a coyote
spread-eagled on the highway
the headless snake
still rippling silver-green
the doe   leg broken   eyes vacant
her stench following the car
or from the bird I hit
that flounders
in the rearview mirror
I will not look away
from my face
by the roadside

The Dilettante

Waterloo, Iowa
The '60s
I was a fresh teacher
just married
had a baby in a year.
Then Indiana—grad school—
studied Anglo-Saxon,
the day Kennedy died
astonished out loud
at someone's *Naked Lunch*
underneath the classroom seat.
Had Hawthorne and James for seminars,
earned *The Scarlet Letter.*
In Columbia, Missouri,
students gave me books—
Dandelion Wine, I and Thou,
Irrational Man,
Stranger in a Strange Land.
Spent hours at The Ivanhoe
listening to The Sound Farm.
Met Bill the librarian
who said he was born ugly
did the talking blues
and loaned me money.
Met Fred the addict
who identified
with *Portnoy's Complaint*
and roared me past
my husband's house
on a Triumph 650.
Tried acid and mescaline—
saw an avocado breathe
saw my problems all at once

saw God through green chiffon
accompanied by Beethoven
and my 30th birthday.
And you, Janis, you too were
acting it all out
saying you fucked them all.
When you died
I hardly knew you had been singing.
I thought you had been screaming.

A Flower Decides to Bloom in My House

The geranium elbows the window,
shoves loud orange to the winter sun.

The coleus stretches its speckled leaves,
offers five blue fingers that last for weeks.

The Norfolk pine grows a nub at its zenith.

The barrel cactus does a shiva—
six prickly arms to the light.

The purple heart licks moisture from the air
with orchid tongues.

The hibiscus opens its red silk fans—
a woman twirling her skirts.

There is nothing scientific about these occasions.
A flower decides to bloom in my house.

Betsy and Bach

In a '55 Buick Special
named Betsy
Virgil Fox shouts
"Bach is alive!"
In stereo
the organ strikes
Tocatta and Fugue in D Minor
and blows my ear
into a gourd
big as Betsy.
I am pushed
to her dome.
I take up
the whole car—
like a roasting marshmallow
I puff out my chest
and scoop out the windows.
Betsy's chrome boobs
are mine.
Greg grins
and drives hard.
Full of Bach
we loom large
down the highway.

Brenda, You Are So Sane

You are not my friend Jeanie
who hides in her house
when we visit
and imagines I am a green witch.
You are not my sister
in a fetal pose
on the bathroom rug
trying to make her anger go away.
You are not my mother
her face a sly secret
announcing my poems to her friends
in baby talk.
You are the woman
who coaches girls' soccer,
sews costumes for a team at the Y,
the woman worried about money
for kids' clothes,
who will go back to school
as soon as she can.
You are the woman who laughs
catching your daughter
with her tongue stuck out
like a gargoyle behind your back.
You are the woman
who wanted to give her first child
to his father and leave
but stayed,
had another baby,
and now sits in this Texas livingroom
curing me of crazy women.

Close in a Double Bed

Close in a double bed
two people sleep.
Back to warm back
they web their body heat.
His elbow rests on her side.
Her toes fill the hollow
behind his knee.
Sometime in the night
they will unfold their arms and legs
and turn toward
but they face away to dream.

In the Garden

"You have an apple butt," my sister says,
and bends her pear over
to weed green beans.
"I get my fingernails dirty
when I weed," she says, "but plants
love attention. I hover around
even if they don't need weeding.
Often Daddy's ghost visits,
gives me advice on asparagus.
I keep his roses large
and hum to the Swiss chard.
Plants grow better with attention.
And if this man doesn't work out,
I'm turning to a woman,
not a feminine woman
like my friend Mary,
but someone masculine enough
to haul manure and fix cars—
a woman, you know, like a man
I can trust."

My Sister's Leather Bag

Like a large patched kidney bean
it hangs pendulous from her shoulder,
an extra breast five years old,
restitched four times—
my sister pulls out piece by piece
a decade of her life.

a 1966 Indiana University student I.D.

a recent letter from Mother
so she won't misinterpret
when she sees her

the letter from her freshman English teacher
a Scorpio—the first person she trusted
who opened her up
called her to his office
to discuss *Romeo and Juliet*

the letter from Steve—
whose last name she can't remember—
who said Come to Hawaii
at his expense

A Family Pact—a way for her and her daughters and John
to have their own spaces
in a large dome
with no doors
They spent a year in weekly rap sessions

addresses—the guy who made her stained glass windows
            the potter who made her dishes
            John's sister's Evansville address

a Food Coop. list
a seed list
and garden layout—
       when to add lime to the soil

an old telephone bill
the last water bill she was looking for
John's bid for sanding
her red oak floors
       deducting $3.00 for beer
           $2.50 per meal
           plus four hours of unidentified
               unexplained
               labor

4 pens, 2 pencils, 1 pair sunglasses, 1 lipstick, 1 chapstick,
Carousel ticket stub, 2 hair twists, 1 comb she can never find

receipt for beads to make jewelry

receipt for lumber
for the gazebo

receipts for hauling pigshit
          horseshit
          cowshit
          bullshit for the garden

her original design for the stained glass windows

a Gideon Book of Psalms
from a Jesus freak

a Golden Savings account book
with $00.00 balance

a prescription for 60 uppers
          30 downers

a broken watch—she likes the bracelet,
                the hand-tooled, painted leather

letter from Mother about John:
        "I think it would be good
        to take a rest from John
        and work on yourself
        as an individual separately—
        you are a beautiful, intelligent
        loving person."

17 matchbooks—she has a fear of being cold—
one of these days they won't be free

bobbypins in a plastic case
she can never find when she needs them

nail kit, emery board, nail file

letter from John when she was
visiting Mother in Arizona:
        "You're loosening up—it will
        benefit everyone—I want to see
        a happy spontaneous you always.
        I hope my presence
        in and out of your life
        will lead to this unfolding . . ."

Silent Unity Prayer for Protection
which Mother sent
when John was going crazy

the note from John
the morning he slipped
acid in her orange juice
before she left
to teach school:

"I am me, I can spark someone else—
I weigh 175 pounds
yet I am
the entire cosmic consciousness . . ."

contract for getting John's ass out of here:
       "I, Julie Hennessy, hereby acknowledge
       a debt of $1,000 to John Hines
       to be paid in full by Dec. 15, 1975,
       subject to the following conditions . . ."

copy of restraining order
       and eviction notice

on the back of a 2nd grade math worksheet
conditions for living with John again:
       "Partnership—
              food and utilities split
              cut wood
              fix leaks
              work in garden
              help can
       own money for drugs and beer
       split costs on visits to family
              except when Mother pays"

Last Will and Testament
with John written out:
"The girls inherit everything,
and after their death half
goes to Crystal and half to
the Theological Science Society
       for Positive Thinking and Meditation

Cremation—body ashes
buried on the woods property
with a self-impregnating
Lone Star cherry tree
planted over them . . ."

Nana

1.
She loved purple.
On her sun porch
we rocked
as she sewed a purple suit
and a pillbox hat to match.

A soft star
in the pulpit—
her black robes,
white hair—
an ordained Methodist minister—
in the churchpew below
when I was a child
I thought she was God.

She was a buyer at Macy's
worked her way
through Moody Bible College.

2.
She loved grandfather.
They held hands
at Sunday dinners.

But when I married
she confessed
"Your grandfather is a good man
but he doesn't understand
someone like me
weak in the flesh."

3.

When he died
and all her friends were dying,
"I love God
but why
has He left me
so alone?"

Not even 24
vitamins-a-day
saved her
from a broken hip
and the Medical Facility.
"Nana, is there nothing
I can do?"
"Bring my Black Strap molasses
and take me home."

We paused at the window—
"See that red horse way out there?"
In the distance
a red oil pump
bending/rising—
bending/rising—
"Every morning," she said,
"he gallops here
to take me home."

Nana at 89
under the oxygen tent
the hospital sheet
caught on the bedpost,
for the first time
I saw her naked—
her maidenhair
ash-blond
as the month she knew
she was a woman.

Woman Found in Art Gallery

I soothe myself on Kline's wide rocking chair brush strokes.

I learn to dance like Franz Marc's "Red Deer" arching their long necks.

I am as supple as the bronze woman "Ille de France."

I move like Jackson Pollock's swirls with liquid pauses.

I am as unselfconscious as Degas' "Woman Bathing,"

as unafraid of being plain as his ladies trying hats,

as casual as Cassatt's "Lydia Leaning on Her Arms."

I do not mind posing as Renoir's "Large Bather."

When I make love my bones go soft like Tanguy's "...Risk of the Sun."

In my person I see every angle of Charles Ross' "Prism."

I am "Infinity Light," "Hybrid Form No. 1."

For each person I have loved Louise Nevelson makes a niche in wood.

I am one of Miro's "Women at Sunrise"

whose head tilts at a right angle

when I know what I mean.

Prufrock Was Wrong

Cecilia is resigned
that another man will leave her
to be "free to love all women."
I know she thinks if she's so beautiful
how come she's alone.
I have Greg who loves me
even though he knows me.
I take it in, feel very solid—very lucky.
And then fall in love with a Persian
whose dark eyes light up
when I enter a room.
And Cecilia leaves Carl for another potter
whose blue eyes light up
when she enters a room.
What we have here is a series of eyes
lighting up in a room.
Prufrock was wrong.
This is the way the women come and go.
They never mention Michelangelo.

The Glass Stem

If I feel the glass stem of this goblet
the bell shape of the top
will the full rim contain you?
When the sun ambers
the tree at my window
will the leaves shout
where you are?
If I read this book, this story
will the words say anything
worth keeping?
If in my mind alone
I touch you
will what I feel
be you
or me?

Duchamp's Nude

All those oiled bones
coming down the staircase
where the eye waits
for the smooth sureness of each limb
the round sharp of that hip bone
the one my friend has
a good wild bone

Burial

Friend,
Lie you by me
in the grey crevices
furrowed like a winter tree.
Lie you by me
in the rectangle humid and soft
our faces damp against the dirt.
I leave you there
as you leave me.
We get up separately
find our ways
to other fine and private places.
We need no wood box
no prayer, no song.
The trees hush the extraneous
as the quietness between us did.
Sometimes I climb the willow and call for you.
Sometimes I hear your voice in the evergreen.

It Must Be Time for Something

The tiger lilies
trumpet their orange.
It must be time for something.
It is time for the cat
to merge his yellow with their orange,
to come home
and time for the dogs
to come home loud and dazzled from their run,
and time for you to come home
a sea-salt, hitch-hiking, sun-burned bloom.

Crystal MacLean Field taught poetry writing and English at Penn Valley Community College in Kansas City from 1971 until her death in 1987. In her home, in the neighborhood south of the University of Missouri-Kansas City campus, she convened the Communiversity Poetry Writing Seminar for many years, influencing and encouraging a large group of area poets. She also participated in the National Endowment for the Art's Poets-in-the-Schools program and the Artists-in-the-Schools program for the Missouri Arts Council. Her poems appeared in many magazines, including *Bloodroot, Dacotah Territory, New Letters*, and *The Mid-America Poetry Review*. Crystal MacLean Field is the author of *The Good Woman* (BkMk Press, 1977) and *My Sister's Leather Bag* (Mid-America Press, 1982). In her memory, The Crystal Field Scholarship in Poetry annually supports a creative-writing student at the University of Missouri-Kansas City.

Colophon

Body text for this book was composed in Garamond Font Bureau, and printed on 60 pound Cougar natural paper, in a limited edition printed by Document Solutions, University of Missouri-Kansas City. The cover is set in Mona Lisa and Myriad Pro, with a background, screened photograph titled "Grassland, 2006" by Jon Scott Anderson.